AF801170

The Small Business That Could™ For Women
MWF Publishing

Book and cover layout and design
by Marna Friedman

Other books by Marna Friedman
The Small Business That Could™
EVENTually Perfect

Foreword

The Small Business That Could™ series of books is dedicated to all small business owners that accept the struggles and frustrations of today - and dreams of tomorrow! May the pages of this book travel with you on your way.

Dear Small Business Owner, and "sister",
this particular book is for you!

Thank you,
Marna Friedman

Some of the pages of this book provide a website address and a brief description of the services that may help you. Many of them will ask you to sign in. I have provided space on a number of pages for you to record your user ID and password. A word to the wise ... passwords should not be written down but coded. Just remember to be consistent in the system you choose!

We all spend countless hours searching for information. This book has been designed with a notes section on several pages for you to write down anything you need to. Use this book as a reference tool.

Mapping your way ....

Pink & Green Do Blend

Women have come a long way. And as we try to determine whether we can have it all, we move forward. The statistics are staggering.

In 2006, there were about 10.4 million businesses owned by women, employing 12.8 million people and generating $1.9 trillion in annual sales.*

Women entrepreneurs are as likely as men to adopt new technology and more likely (24% vs. 18%) than women in general.*

Women start their own business at 1.5 times the rate of men.*

So the statistics show that women are successfully venturing into the business arena. Pink ladies and green money blend nicely together. Yet unlike the adage about men, we do read maps and like to follow directions. So here are some directions to find your way through the internet and hopefully to help you succeed in your endeavor. Since many of these sites offer information in multiple categories, they are in alphabetical order. A "tag cloud" by tag category follows for easy reference. A directory of networking

My Notes

organizations is broken down by state. The final section of this book is dedicated to the many aspects of business you may seek help with.

*National Numbers: Women-Owned Businesses in the United States 2006." Center for Women's Business Research. Accessed: April 23, 2008

Follow the Rules

There are many federal agencies available to assist small businesses, whether they are women owned or not. The IRS, SBA and other government agency websites offer a tremendous amount of information and assistance for small businesses.

Copyright Office

http://www.copyright.gov

Internal Revenue Service

http://www.irs.gov

Offical Business Link to the US Government

http://www.business.gov

Small Business Administration

http://www.sba.gov

Social Security for Self-Employed

http://www.ssa.gov

My Notes

My Notes

United States Patent and Trademark Office

http://www.uspto.gov

Women Business

http://www.womenbiz.gov

For Women Only

WBE stands for Woman Business Enterprise and the certification denotes that a woman (or women) has majority ownership and control of the business. Note that WBE certification has no bearing on any form of endorsement for the business.

So why is WBE certification important?
Most government purchasing agencies track their business with women business owners. Having this certification is the only way these agencies can confirm that you are indeed a woman owned business. Most other corporations also track this information and rely on the MBE certification.

The Women's Equity in Contracting Act (2000) stipulates a federal goal, currently 5%, to restrict competition for women-owned firms that have WBE certification, up to 5% of all contracts (http://www.giveme5.com).

My Notes

My Notes

Certification Criteria

1. Woman must own and control at least 51% of the business
2. Woman owner must be a US citizen or legal resident
3. Woman owner must serve as President or CEO (if both positions exist)
4. Woman must have ownership and officer position for at least six months
5. Woman owner must be active in daily management

Money for Women

While women are not considered a minority, there are special programs to help women possibly secure financing for their businesses. The following websites offer information on programs that are exclusive to women.

http://www.count-me-in.org/

http://www.digitalwomengrants.org/

http://www.goldenseeds.com/home/

http://iiwomen.com/

https://www.key.com/

http://www.wfnet.org/

http://www.womensnet.net/

http://www.wvf-ny.org/#

My Notes

My Notes

The following states offer programs that may provide financial assistance to women entrepreneurs.

CA: Women's Economic Ventures Small Business Loan Fund

http://www.wevonline.org/get-a-loan/overview

DE: Access Program

http://dedo.delaware.gov/Access.shtml

IL: Minority, Women & Disabled Participation Loan Program

http://www.commerce.state.il.us/

IA: Target Small Business Assistance Program

http://www.iowalifechanging.com/business/tsb.aspx

MA: BDC Capital Community Laons

http://www.mass-business.com/

MS: Capital Access Loan Program

http://www.mississippi.org/index.php?id=278

NJ: Urban Plus

http://www.njeda.com/web/Aspx_pg/Templates

NM: The Loan Fund

http://www.loanfund.org/

NY: Micro Loans for Minority & Women Owned Businesses

http://www.nylovesmwbe.ny.gov/

WI: Linked Deposit Loan Subsidy

http://www.wheda.com/

WI: Women's Business Initiative Corporation Small Business Loans

http://www.wheda.com/

My Notes

Associations

Women, unlike men, emphasize relationship building and fact gathering when running a company. Also, women are more likely to consult with employees and fellow business associates before making a major decision.

So before you even venture through the many internet sites that can help you...reach out to your peers. For this reason, the first pages of this book are dedicated to the many associations offering help to women entrepreneurs.

My Notes

My Notes

http://www.abwa.org/

AMERICAN BUSINESS WOMEN'S ASSOCIATION
Brings together businesswomen of
diverse occupations to provide opportunities
for them to help themselves and others
grow personally and professionally
through leadership; education,
networking support and national recognition.

Login Information

User ID ______________________

Password ______________________

http://www.athenafoundation.org/

Athena International
Supporting, developing and honoring
women leaders while inspiring women
to achieve their full potential
and create balance in leadership worldwide.

Login Information

User ID ______________________

Password ______________________

My Notes

My Notes

http://www.awbc.biz/

ASSOCIATION OF WOMEN'S BUSINESS CENTERS
Supports entrepreneurial development among women as a way to achieve economic self-sufficiency, create wealth and participate in economic development through education, training, mentoring, business development and financing opportunities.

Login Information

User ID ______________________

Password ______________________

http://www.bpwfoundation.org/

BUSINESS AND PROFESSIONAL WOMEN'S FOUNDATION
Supports workforce development programs
and workplace policies that recognize
the diverse needs of working women,
communities and businesses.

Login Information

User ID ____________________

Password ____________________

My Notes

My Notes

http://www.ceowomen.org/

CREATING ECONOMIC OPPORTUNITIES FOR WOMEN

The mission of C.E.O. Women is to create economic opportunities for low-income immigrant and refugee women through teaching English, communications and entrepreneurship skills, so they can establish successful livelihoods.

Login Information

User ID ____________________

Password ____________________

http://www.fcem.org/

WORLD ASSOCIATION OF WOMEN ENTREPRENEURS
Brings together in solidarity and friendship,
like-minded women who share a common interest,
that of entrepreneurship

Login Information

User ID ______________________________

Password ______________________________

My Notes

My Notes

http://www.nafe.com/

NATIONAL ASSOCIATION FOR FEMALE EXECUTIVES
Provides education, networking, and
public advocacy to empower its members
to achieve career success and financial security.

Login Information

User ID ______________________

Password ______________________

http://naofp.com/

NATIONAL ASSOCIATION OF FEMALE PROFESSIONALS
An organization that provides its members with networking, consulting, and educational opportunities to advance their careers and enrich their professional lives

Login Information

User ID ______________________________

Password ______________________________

My Notes

My Notes

http://www.nawbo.org/

NATIONAL ASSOCIATION OF WOMEN BUSINESS OWNERS
A one-stop resource to help propel
women business owners
into greater economic, social
and political spheres of power worldwide.

Login Information

User ID ______________________________

Password ______________________________

http://owit.org/

ORGANIZATION OF WOMEN IN INTERNATIONAL TRADE
A non-profit professional organization designed to promote women doing business in international trade by providing networking and educational opportunities.

Login Information

User ID ____________________

Password ____________________

My Notes

My Notes

http://uswcc.org/

U.S. Women's Chamber of Commerce
Through its members, the USWCC unifies
the collective strength of women to leverage
their position as the "most influential
economic force in America".

Login Information

User ID ____________________

Password ____________________

http://www.we-inc.org/

WOMEN ENTREPRENEURS
As a project of the
Small Business & Entrepreneurship Council
(SBE Council), WE Inc. aim is to
improve and enhance the economic climate
for women's entrepreneurship

Login Information

User ID ______________________________

Password ______________________________

My Notes

My Notes

http://www.wiit.org/

NATIONAL ASSOCIATION OF WOMEN IN INTERNATIONAL TRADE
Provides educational and networking opportunities to professional women involved in international trade and business.

Login Information

User ID ______________________

Password ______________________

http://www.wipp.org/

WOMEN IMPACTING PUBLIC POLICY

A national bi-partisan public policy organization
that advocates for and on behalf of women and minorities
in business in the legislative processes of our nation,
creating economic opportunities and building bridges
and alliances to other small business organizations

Login Information

User ID ____________________

Password ____________________

My Notes

My Notes

http://www.womensleadershipexchange.com/

WOMEN'S LEADERSHIP EXCHANGE

A social entrepreneurship organization that
recognizes the unique challenges facing women in business.
WLE offers a program that
helps them fill the information gap and
provides a venue for building connections
that will facilitate their success in business and in life.

Login Information

User ID ______________________________

Password ______________________________

Moving On and Reaching Out

As women and sisters, we form instant bonds that help us to build ourselves up and work together. Many of us have attended meetings where we are extremely outnumbered by men. Decades after the feminist movement, we are still struggling with glass ceilings and business opportunities.

Many of us accept the traditional networking opportunities and struggle to find our own voice. The sites that follow were developed to help us, women, in our quest to succeed in business. Every effort has been made to include all sites, but the internet is everchanging.

My Notes

My Notes

http://www.blogher.com/

a community to help create opportunities
for women who blog to pursue exposure,
education, community, and
economic empowerment

Login Information

User ID ______________________

Password ______________________

Tags: blog, conference

http://www.buildanest.com/

connecting women through
art, craft and opportunity.

Login Information

User ID ______________________________

Password ______________________________

Tags: ecommerce, online store

My Notes

My Notes

http://count-me-in.org/

provides resources for business loans
and educational scholarships for women.

Login Information

User ID ____________________

Password ____________________

Tags: laons, scholarships

http://www.digitalwomen.org/

an international network for women in business
designed to provide business resources,
small business loan information and
support for businesswomen worldwide.

Login Information

User ID ______________________

Password ______________________

Tags: grants, laons, small business tools

My Notes

My Notes

http://www.divatoolbox.com/

empower, educate, and entertain women

Login Information

User ID ______________________________

Password ______________________________

Tags: networking, radio show

http://www.enterprisingwomen.com/

a magazine providing a friendly meeting place, a public forum, and a national stage for the critical issues confronting women's businesses and daily lives from the unique perspectives and experiences of entrepreneurial women.

Login Information

User ID ______________________________

Password ______________________________

Tags: awards, magazine

My Notes

My Notes

http://entrepreneurette.com/

a place for you to connect
with other women in business,
network and build your business.

Login Information

User ID ____________________

Password ____________________

Tags: blog, forum, networking, web 2.0

http://www.etsy.com/

enables people to make a living making things,
and to reconnect makers with buyers.
Their vision is to build a new economy
and present a better choice.

Login Information

User ID ______________________________

Password ______________________________

Tags: blog, , e-commerce, online store

My Notes

My Notes

http://ewnsfo.ning.com/

social network offering techniques and support
to market, pitch and GROW your business!

Login Information

User ID ____________________

Password ____________________

Tags: blog, , conferences, events, resources, social network

http://www.ewomennetwork.com/

provides hosting on dedicated services as well as website management

My Notes

Login Information

User ID ______________________________

Password ______________________________

Tags: blog, , conferences, radio show, resource

My Notes

http://www.flokka.com/

a place to create your own blog,
or add your existing blog - and share your voice,
and your business with the world

Login Information

User ID ____________________

Password ____________________

Tags: blog, forum

http://fuzzb.com/

a social network where you can
buy, sell, and create without limits,
become a part of something extraordinary
changing the social selling planet

Login Information

User ID ______________________

Password ______________________

Tags: e-commerce, onlinestore, social networking

My Notes

My Notes

http://www.theheartlinknetwork.com/

an all access pass to success that so
many women dream about.
It is a networking tool that
aids women in growing and expanding
their businesses while they strengthen
their community.

Login Information

User ID ____________________

Password ____________________

Tags: networking

http://herbigidea.com/

an inspiring place for women bloggers, business owners, poduct inventors, podcasters, PR, marketing and ad reps, authors, musicians, and those who dream of owning a business.

Login Information

User ID ______________________

Password ______________________

Tags: blog, networking, podcasts, public relations, resources.

My Notes

My Notes

http://www.herstartup.com/

helps women launch & grow their businesses and give back. By doing so, we help women lead more integrated lives, end the age old struggle between work that matters vs. that which pays the bills, and enable them to do more than focus solely on the bottom line.

Login Information

User ID ______________________

Password ______________________

Tags: networking, resources, small business tools, training

http://www.thejoyofconnecting.com/

a non-membership organization
to support women entrepreneurs,
business owners, and other professional women.

Login Information

User ID ______________________

Password ______________________

Tags: networking

My Notes

My Notes

http://www.ladieswholaunch.com/

offers resources and connections,
for business, for life and helps make
entrepreneurship accessible to any woman
with a project, dream or aspiration to
start her own business and be successful.

Login Information

User ID ______________________

Password ______________________

Tags: conferences, networking, small business tools, training

http://www.littlepinkbook.us.com/

an interactive community for women in business offering a unique blend of social networking, peer-to-peer support, personal development, online learning resources, leadership positioning, and infinite possibilities

Login Information

User ID ______________________________

Password ______________________________

Tags: mentoring, social networking, training

My Notes

My Notes

http://mywomanownedbusiness.com/

a space for women business owners to gather,
to share ideas, to offer solutions
and to inspire one another

Login Information

User ID ______________________

Password ______________________

Tags: blog, chat,, ecommerce, networking

https://the-office.com/womens-network/

a networking resource for
women executives/professionals.

Login Information

User ID ______________________________

Password ______________________________

Tags: networking

My Notes

My Notes

http://www.pinklinx.com/

mentoring, networking
and social opportunities abound in the
various chat rooms, groups and blogs
that are made available on the site and women
from all over the world are readily accessible to
each other with just a click

Login Information

User ID ______________________________

Password ______________________________

Tags: blog, chat rooms, mentoring, networking

http://powernetwork.ning.com/

a place for business to happen.
This is a business network of entrepreneurs
and business professionals.

Login Information

User ID ______________________________

Password ______________________________

Tags: blog, social networking

My Notes

My Notes

http://www.savorthesuccess.com/

offers a boutique, social network and
PR Co-Op for female entrepreneurs
& professionals.

Login Information

User ID ______________________

Password ______________________

Tags: blog, networking, online store, public relations

http://www.shefinds.com/

studies the trends and surfs the web
for the best items and then sends you a link
in the SheFinds weekly newsletter

Login Information

User ID ______________________________

Password ______________________________

Tags: coupons, fashion, newsletter

My Notes

My Notes

http://shesconnected.com/

destination for today's busy woman.
Now managing daily activities, planning events
and coordinating your commitments
is easier than ever!

Login Information

User ID ______________________________

Password ______________________________

Tags: events, networking, planning

http://societyofsocialpreneurs.ning.com/

a network of individuals who utilizes social means
to promote their business, services
or creative works.

Login Information

User ID ______________________________

Password ______________________________

Tags: blog, planning, social networking

My Notes

My Notes

http://teamwomen.com/

a business networking organization
by women,
for women

Login Information

User ID ____________________

Password ____________________

Tags: networking

http://twitterqueens.ning.com/

empowering women in the understanding
and use of emerging social media techniques.
That's what she twittered.

Login Information

User ID ______________________________

Password ______________________________

Tags: social media, social networking, twitter

My Notes

My Notes

http://www.wbenc.org/

nation's leading advocate of women-owned businesses as suppliers to America's corporations. It also is the largest third-party certifier of businesses owned and operated by women in the United States.

Login Information

User ID ______________________

Password ______________________

Tags: certification, networking, training

http://we-inc.org/

a project of the Small Business &
Entrepreneurship Council (SBE Council) --
a prominent advocacy and research organization
dedicated to protecting small business
and promoting entrepreneurship

Login Information

User ID ______________________

Password ______________________

Tags: networking, resources

My Notes

My Notes

http://womanowned.com/

provides the information, tools,
networking opportunities and advice
that have helped hundreds of thousands of women.

Login Information

User ID ______________________

Password ______________________

Tags: networking, resources, small business tools

http://womenbusinessowners.ning.com/

educates, empowers, and enhances the lives of women business owners and children throughout the world.

Login Information

User ID ____________________

Password ____________________

Tags: blog, resources, social networking

My Notes

My Notes

http://www.womencorp.org/

an international company that provides
high quality experiential learning programs
and leadership development for women in business.

Login Information

User ID ______________________

Password ______________________

Tags: networking, resources, training

http://www.womenempower.com/

a web site for Women, about Women, by Women.
where you can share your experience,
your dreams, your success, and
promote your business all for FREE!

Login Information

User ID ____________________

Password ____________________

Tags: blog, networking, resources

My Notes

My Notes

http://womenofvision.ning.com/

a social networking group for women
to share strategies and ideas for
Home Based Businesses and Internet Marketing.

Login Information

User ID ______________________

Password ______________________

Tags: blog, resources, social networking

http://www.womensbusinessresearch.crg/

provides data-driven knowledge that advances the economic, social and political impact of women business owners and their enterprises

My Notes

Login Information

User ID ______________________

Password ______________________

Tags: research, webinairs

My Notes

http://www.womensnet.net/

finding funding and free grants for
women-owned business.

Login Information

User ID ______________________________

Password ______________________________

Tags: blog, funding, grants, loans, resources

http://www.womenspeernetwork.ning.com/

a social network dedicated to establishing relationships and getting to know as many people as we can, doors start opening and opportunities start presenting themselves.

Login Information

User ID ______________________

Password ______________________

Tags: blog, resources, social networking

My Notes

My Notes

http://womenssmallbiznetwork.ning.com/

a network of creative, motivated women
empowering & supporting each other
in growing & creating incredibly
successful small businesses.

Login Information

User ID ______________________________

Password ______________________________

Tags: blog, social networking

http://womeniiwomen.ning.com/

a social network to support, connect and educate
Women Entrepreneurs as they build
and lead their businesses and corporations
to the next level.

Login Information

User ID ______________________________

Password ______________________________

Tags: chat, funding, resources, social networking

My Notes

My Notes

http://www.wowowow.com/

provides the information, tools,
networking opportunities and advice
that have helped hundreds of thousands of women.

Login Information

User ID ______________________

Password ______________________

Tags: networking, resources

Having It All

According to the National Association for Moms in Business, 44% of women business owners have children under the age of 18 and even more have older children and grandchildren. 61% of female corporate executives also have children, and they are on the rise -- an increase of 60% has been seen in women taking on executive positions. So this book would not be complete without listing sites that are not only exclusive to women in business, but exclusive to moms in business.

My Notes

My Notes

http://www.freelancemom.com/

a support network for women
working from home through a
supportive community rich with
home business ideas and internet marketing
strategies to support you and help you to make
smart decisions from choosing your
business to promoting it.

Login Information

User ID ______________________

Password ______________________

Tags: networking, resources, wahm

http://mibn.org/

NATIONAL ASSOCIATION FOR MOMS IN BUSINESS
a national association representing
entrepreneurial, executive & CEO Moms
through networking and education.

Login Information

User ID ______________________

Password ______________________

Tags: networking, resources, training, wahm

My Notes

My Notes

http://www.momsinbusinessunite.com/

an annual conference that brings together
women and mom business owners
for workshops, new inventor showcase, networking,
award ceremony, resource marketplace,
and childcare to support
and promote the growing number of
women and mom-owned businesses.

Login Information

User ID ______________________

Password ______________________

Tags: conference, networking, resources, training, wahm

.http://www.mompack.com/

moms helping moms in business
to support our mutual goals of success
through an innovative,
free advertising partnership.

Login Information

User ID ______________________

Password ______________________

Tags: moms, networking, resources, wahm

My Notes

My Notes

http://www.momsunitedinbusiness.com/

a social network dedicated to helping
mom entrepreneurs build their businesses
and connect with other moms in business

Login Information

User ID ____________________

Password ____________________

Tags: networking, resources, wahm

http://www.moneymakingmommy.com/

research work at home jobs and opportunities, telecommuting positions, home based business ideas, making money and more.

Login Information

User ID ______________________________

Password ______________________________

Tags: networking, resources, training, wahm

My Notes

My Notes

http://superwomanlifestyle.ning.com/

a social network where you can highlight
and showcase your lifestyle as a
Mom, Partner, Wife, Business Owner, Entrepreneur,
Career-Woman and Overall SUPERWOMAN!

Login Information

User ID ______________________

Password ______________________

Tags: blog, networking, wahm

http://www.wahm.com/

helps you monetize your site
with advertising that fits the content
and user base of your site.

Login Information

User ID ______________________

Password ______________________

Tags: networking

My Notes

My Notes

http://womenhomebusiness.com/

presents success stories of of small
and home based women entrepreneurs.

Login Information

User ID ______________________

Password ______________________

Tags: networking, resources, wahm

Tag Cloud

Following is a listing of all websites (p. 28-78) broken down by tag.

Awards

Blog

awards blog certification chat
conference coupons
ecommerce events facebook
fashion forum funding grants
loans magazine mentoring
networking newsletter online
store planning podcasts
public relations radio show research
resources scholarships
small business tools social
networking training twitter
wahm web 2.0

awards blog certification chat conference coupons ecommerce events facebook fashion forum funding grants loans magazine mentoring networking newsletter online store planning podcasts public relations radio show research resources scholarships small business tools social networking training twitter wahm web 2.0

Certification

Chat

Conference

awards blog certification chat conference coupons ecommerce events facebook fashion forum funding grants loans magazine mentoring networking newsletter online store planning podcasts public relations radio show research resources scholarships small business tools social networking training twitter wahm web 2.0

awards blog certification chat conference coupons ecommerce events facebook fashion forum funding grants loans magazine mentoring networking newsletter online store planning podcasts public relations radio show research resources scholarships small business tools social networking training twitter wahm web 2.0

Grants

Loans

Magazine

Mentoring

Networking

awards blog certification chat
conference coupons
ecommerce events facebook
fashion forum funding grants
loans magazine mentoring
networking newsletter online
store planning podcasts
public relations radio show research
resources scholarships
small business tools social
networking training twitter
wahm web 2.0

awards blog certification chat conference coupons ecommerce events facebook fashion forum funding grants loans magazine mentoring networking newsletter online store planning podcasts public relations radio show research resources scholarships small business tools social networking training twitter wahm web 2.0

awards blog certification chat
conference coupons
ecommerce events facebook
fashion forum funding grants
loans magazine mentoring
networking newsletter online
store planning podcasts
public relations radio show research
resources scholarships
small business tools social
networking training twitter
wahm web 2.0

awards blog certification chat conference coupons ecommerce events facebook fashion forum funding grants loans magazine mentoring networking newsletter online store planning podcasts public relations radio show research resources scholarships small business tools social networking training twitter wahm web 2.0

Scholarships

Small business tools

Social media

Social networking

Training

awards blog certification chat
conference coupons
ecommerce events facebook
fashion forum funding grants
loans magazine mentoring
networking newsletter online
store planning podcasts
public relations radio show research
resources scholarships
small business tools social
networking training twitter
wahm web 2.0

awards blog certification chat
conference coupons
ecommerce events facebook
fashion forum funding grants
loans magazine mentoring
networking newsletter online
store planning podcasts
public relations radio show research
resources scholarships
small business tools social
networking training twitter
wahm web 2.0

Twitter

WAHM

Web 2.0

Webinairs

Throughout the Country

Women throughout the US are working together to help each other start and build their own business. Frequently we need to relocate to other areas of the country for business or personal reasons. Navigating our way through networking opportunities can be overwhelming. The following pages list some of the associations and networking opportunities available to women throughout the country.

Many networking groups for women are in the grassroot stage and do not have easily accessible websites. As you become active in many of the larger networking groups, you will begin to discover others. Any sites marked with an asterik (*) are by invitation only.

You can also checkout http://www.meetup.com/ for other businesswomen networks in your area.

Alabama Alaska Arizona
Arkansas California Colorado
Connecticut Delaware
District of Columbia Florida
Georgia Hawaii Idaho
Illinois Indiana Iowa
Kansas Kentucky
Louisiana Maine Maryland
Massachusetts Michigan
Minnesota Mississippi
Missouri Montana Nebraska
Nevada New Hampshire
New Jersey New Mexico
New York North Carolina Ohio
Oklahoma Oregon
Pennsylvania Rhode Island
South Carolina
Tennessee Texas Utah
Vermont Virginia
Washington West Virginia
Wisconsin Wyoming

My Notes

Alabama

Central Alabama Women's Business Center
http://www.cawbc.org/
Executive Women International - Birmingham
http://www.ewibirmingham.org/
Executive Women International - Huntsville
http://www.ewihsv.org/
Executive Women International - Mobile
http://www.ewiconnect.com/
Executive Women International - Montgomery
http://www.ewiconnect.com/
The Women's Exchange
http://www.womens-exchange.com/
Women's Business Center of North Alabama
http://www.wbcna.org/
Women's Business Center, Inc.
http://womenbiz.biz/
Women Who Mean Business
http://womenwhomeanbusiness.net/

Alaska

Alaska Women's Network

http://www.alaskawomensnetwork.org/

Business & Professional Women/Anchorage

http://bpw-anchorage.org/

Arizona

Arizona Business and Professional Women

http://www.bpwaz.org/

Arizona Business Women

http://www.arizonabusinesswomen.com/

Arizona Business & Professional Women's Foundation

http://www.arizonabpwfoundation.com/

Bisbee Business & Professional Women

http://bpwbisbeeaz.org/

Central Phoenix Women

http://www.centralphoenixwomen.org/

Empowered Women Network

http://www.empoweredwomen.org/

Executive Women International - Phoenix

http://www.ewiphoenix.org/

My Notes

My Notes

Executive Women International - Tuscon
http://www.ewitucson.org/
Little Pink Book
http://www.littlepinkbook.us.com/
Scottsdale Express Network
http://scottsdaleexpress.org/
Women's Network Exchange of Arizona
http://www.wnea.org/

Arkansas

Arkansas Business & Professional Women
http://www.arkansasbpw.org/
Central Arkansas National Association of Women Business Owners
http://www.canawbo.org/
Executive Women International - Little Rock
http://www.ewiconnect.com/
Executive Women International - Northwest Arkansas
http://www.ewinwa.org/
Women in Networking
http://www.winnwa.com/

California

Business and Professional Women CA

http://www.bpwcal.org/

California Direct Selling Women

http://cadirectsellingwomen.ning.com/

California Women

http://www.californiawomen.org/

California Women Business Owners

http://www.cwbo.org/

California Women Partner

http://california.womenpartner.com/

Crave Party - San Francisco

http://www.craveparty.com/

Downtown Women's Club

http://www.downtownwomensclub.com/

Executive Women International - Long Beach

http://www.ewilongbeach.org/

Executive Women International - Los Angeles

http://www.executivewomenla.org/

Executive Women International - Pomona Valley

www.ewipv.com/

My Notes

My Notes

Executive Women International - San Diego
http://www.ewisandiego.org/
Executive Women International - San Fernando Valley
http://www.ewisfv.org/
Executive Women International - San Francisco
http://www.ewiconnect.com/
National Association of Women Business Owners - OC
http://www.nawbo-oc.com/
Networking Women Know
http://networkingwomenknow.ning.com/
Pink Passport Society Moonlighters & Multipreneurs
http://pinkpassportsociety.ning.com/
Powerful You
http://powerfulyou.com/
Professional Business Women of California
http://www.pbwc.org/
Professional Women's Network of Southern Claifornia
http://pwnscal.ning.com/
San Francisco Circle
http://sanfranciscocircle.ning.com/main/
South Bay Business Women's Small Business Network
http://southbaybizwomen.ning.com/

Women 2.0
http://www.women2.org/
Women's Business Center of California
http://www.wbcc-sd.org/
Women Empowered in Business - San Francisco
http://websforg.ning.com/

Colorado

Boulder Business & Professional Women
http://www.boulderbpw.org/
Boulder Mom's Town
http://bouldermomstown.ning.com/
Business Women's Connection
http://www.businesswomensconnection.com/
Colorado Business & Professional Women's Foundation
http://www.cbpwef.org/
Colorado Women's Chamber of Commerce
http://www.cwcc.org/
Executive Women International - Colorado Springs
http://www.springsewi.com/
Executive Women International - Denver
http://www.ewidenver.org/

My Notes

My Notes

Powerful You
http://powerfulyou.com/
Women Entrepreneur to Entrepreneur
http://we2eboulder.ning.com/
Women's Resource Center
http://www.wrcdurango.org/

Connecticut

Central Connecticut Women's Forum*
http://centralctwomen.ning.com/
Connecticut Women's Business Development Center
http://www.ctwbdc.org/
Entrepreneurial Women's Network
http://www.ewn-ct.org/
National Association of Women Business Owners CT
http://www.nawboct.org/
Powerful You
http://powerfulyou.com/

Delaware

Business & Professional Women of Delaware
http://www.bpwdelaware.org/
Business Womens Network DE
http://www.bwnde.com/
Delaware Women's Conference
http://www.delawarewomen.org/
Her Biz
http://www.herbiz.net/
National Association of Women Business Owners DE
http://www.nawbodelaware.org/
News 4 Women
http://www.news4women.org/
Office of Minority & Women Enterprise
http://omwbe.delaware.gov/
Powerful You
http://powerfulyou.com/
Wilmington Women in Business
http://www.wwb.org/

My Notes

My Notes

District of Columbia

DC Web Women
http://www.dcwebwomen.org/
Downtown Women's Club
http://www.downtownwomensclub.com/
Executive Women International - DC
http://www.ewi-dc.org/
Lipstick Rocks
http://www.loudounwng.com/

Florida

Executive Women International - Orlando
http://www.ewiorlando.com/
Executive Women International - Tampa Bay
http://www.ewi-tampa.com/
Executive Women of the Palm Beaches Social Network
http://executivewomen.ning.com/
Florida Business Style
http://floridabizstyle.ning.com/
Florida Federation of Business & Professional Women's Clubs
http://www.bpwfl.org/

Florida Women in Business
http://www.fwib.org/
Florida Women Partner
http://florida.womenpartner.com/
Florida Womens Business Center
http://www.flwbc.org/
Jacksonville Women Business Owners
http://www.jaxwbo.org/
Kerry's Network for Women
http://www.kerrysnetworkforwomen.com/
Orlando Business Women
http://www.orlandobusinesswomen.org/
Powerful You
http://powerfulyou.com/
Space Coast Women
http://spacecoastwomen.ning.com/
Women's Business Center
http://womensbusinesscenter.ning.com/
Women's Independent Networking Group Service
http://wingsofjacksonville.ning.com/

My Notes

My Notes

Georgia

Atlanta Area Council American Business Womens Association

http://www.aacabwa.org/

Business Women's Network of North Georgia

http://www.business-womens-network.org/

Crave Party - Atlanta

http://www.craveparty.com/

Downtown Women's Club

http://www.downtownwomensclub.com/

Executive Women International - Atlanta

http://www.ewiabq.org/

Georgia Executive Women's Network

http://www.gewn.org/

Georgia Federation of Business & Professional Womens Clubs

http://georgiaprofessionalwomen.com/

Greater Women's Business Council

http://www.gwbc.biz/

NationalAssociation of Women Business Owners - Atlanta

http://www.nawboatlanta.org/

Startup Chicks

http://www.startupchicks.net/

Tri-State Business Women
http://www.tri-statebusinesswomen.com/
Women About Business
http://www.womenaboutbiz.com/
Women Intelligently Networking
http://www.win-atl.com/
Women of Gwinnett Business Networking*
http://womenofgwinnett.ning.com/

Hawaii

Executive Women International- Honolulu
http://www.ewihonolulu.org/
Hawaii Womens Business Center
http://www.hwbc.org/
Women's Fund of Hawaii
http://womensfundhawaii.org/

Idaho

Executive Women International - Boise
http://www.ewiconnect.com/

My Notes

My Notes

Idaho Business Womens Network
http://www.ibwn.biz/
Idaho Professional Women Enterprise Network
http://www.ipwen.org/

Illinois

Association of Business Women - Chicago
http://www.abwa-chicago.org/
Batavia Women in Business
http://www.bataviawib.com/
Business & Professional Women - Charleston
http://www.bpwcharleston.com/
Business & Professional Women - IL
http://www.bpw-il.org/
Business Womens Ebtrepreneur Network
http://businesswomennetwork.ning.com/
Chicagoland Incubator
http://chicagolandincubator.ning.com/
Crave Party - Chicago
http://www.craveparty.com/
Executive Womenn International - Chicago
http://www.ewichicago.org/

National Association of Women Business Owners - Central IL
http://www.nawbo-cil.org/
Powerful You
http://powerfulyou.com/
Professional Business Women
http://www.pbwi.net/
Professional Women's Network
http://www.pwncentral.com/
Women's Business Development Center
http://www.wbdc.org/
Women in Networking - Lake Zurich
http://www.winlz.com/

Indiana

Central Indiana Business Womens Center
http://www.nsibiz.org/
Executive Women International - Fort Wayne
http://www.ewiconnect.com/
Executive Women International - Indianapolis
http://www.indyewi.org/
Indaiana Business Women
http://www.indianabusinesswomen.org/

My Notes

My Notes

Indana Business & Professional Women
http://www.indianabpwfoundation.org/
National Association of Women Business Owners - INDY
http://www.nawboindy.org/
Network of Women in Business
http://www.nowib.com/
Tri-State Women
http://tri-statewomen.ning.com/

Iowa

Executive Women International - Des Moines
http://www.ewidsm.org/
Iowa's Women Conference
http://www.iowawomensconference.com/
Metro Women's Network
http://mwniowa.org/
National Association of Women Business Owners - Central Iowa
http://www.nawbo-ci.org/
Women Supporting Women in Business
http://womensupportingwomen.ning.com/

Kansas

Business & Professional Women of Kansas
http://www.bpwkansas.org/

Executive Women International - Kansas City
http://www.ewiconnect.com/

Executive Women International - Wichita
http://www.ewiconnect.com/

Flourish
http://www.toflourish.com/

Kansas City Council of Women Business Owners
http://www.kc-cwbo.org/

Kansas Womens Business Center
http://www.kansaswbc.com/

Kentucky

Executive Women International - Cincinnati/Northern Kentucky
http://www.ewicincinnatinky.com/

Executive Women International - Louisville
http://www.ewiconnect.com/

Kentucky Federation of Business & Professional Women
http://www.bpw-ky.org/

My Notes

My Notes

National Association of Women Business Owners - Lexington
http://www.lexnawbo.org/
National Association of Women Business Owners - Louisville
http://www.nawbolouisville.org/
Professional Womens Forum
http://www.professionalwomensforum.com/
Women Leading Kentucky
http://www.womenleadingky.com/

Louisiana

Enterprise Consofrtium of the Gulf Coast Womens Business Center
http://www.ecgcwbc.com/
Executive Women International - Baton Rouge
http://www.ewi.com/
Executive Women International - New Orleans
http://www.ewiconnect.com/
Executive Women International - Shreveport-Bossier City
http://www.ewi-shreveport-bossier.org/
National Association of Women Business Owners - NO
http://www.nawbo-no.org/
Powerful You
http://powerfulyou.com/

WOMEN'S MARKETPLACE OF BATON ROUGE
http://brmarketplace.ning.com/

Maine

MAINE CENTERS FOR WOMEN, WORK AND COMMUNITY
http://www.womenworkandcommunity.org/
MAINE WOMEN BUSINESS OWNERS
http://www.wbcmaine.org/
MAINE WOMENS FUND
http://www.mainewomensfund.org/
MAINE WOMENS NETWORK
http://www.mainewomensnetwork.com/
MAINE WOMENS POLICY CENTER
http://www.mainewomenspolicycenter.org/
NEW ENGLAND WOMEN BUSINESS OWNERS
http://www.newbo.org/

Maryland

AMERICAN BUSINESS WOMENS ASSOCIATION - MD
http://www.abwamdcap.org/

My Notes

My Notes

Business & Professional Womens Network - MD
http://www.bpwmaryland.org/
Business Women's Network of Howard County
http://www.bwn-hoco.org/
Chesapeake Professional Womens Network
http://www.cpwnet.org/
Women Business Owners
http://www.wbo.org/
Women Entrepreneurs of Baltimore
http://www.webinc.org/
Women in Harmony
http://www.womeninharmony.org/
Women Business Owners of Montgomery County
http://www.wbo-mc.com/
Womens Expo
http://www.womensexpomd.com/

Massachusetts

Berkshire Business & Professional Women
http://bbpw.net/
Boston Women's Network
http://www.bostonwomensnetwork.org/

Center for Women & Enterprise
http://www.cweboston.org/
Crave Party - Boston
http://www.craveparty.com/
Downtown Women's Club
http://www.downtownwomensclub.com/
The Glass Hammer
http://www.theglasshammer.com/
Massachusetts Federation of Business & Professional Women
http://www.mabpw.org/
National Association of Business & Professional Women - Boston
http://www.nawboboston.com/
New England Women Business Owners
http://www.newbo.org/
Professional Women in Massachusetts
http://profwomen.ning.com/
South Shore Women's Business Network
http://www.sswbn.org/
State Office of Minority & Women Business Assistance
http://www.somwba.state.ma.us/
Women in Business Guide
http://www.wibguide.net/

My Notes

My Notes

Women in Business Connection
http://www.wibconnection.org/
Womens Business Network - MA
http://www.wbn-ma.org/
Womens Leadership Exchange
http://www.womensleadershipexchange.com/

Michigan

Business & Professional Women of Michigan
http://www.bpw-michigan.org/
Downtown Women's Club
http://www.downtownwomensclub.com/
Executive Women International - Detroit/Windsor
http://www.ewidetroitwindsor.org/
Michigan Professional Women's Network
http://www.mpwn.org/
Michigan Women's Marketplace
http://www.miwomen.com/
Professional Business Women's Network
http://www.pbwn.org/
Women Business Owners of Southeastern Michigan
http://www.wbo-mich.org/

Women's Division of Leavenworth-Lansing Area Chamber of Commerce
http://pinkpassportsociety.ning.com/

Minnesota

Executive Women International - Minneapolis
http://www.executivewomenmn.org/
Executive Women International - Rochester
http://www.executivewomenmn.org/rochester.html/
Executive Women International - St. Paul
http://www.executivewomenmn.org/
Minnesota Business Women
http://www.mnbusinesswomen.org/
Minnesota Moms in Business
http://www.mnmomsinbusiness.com/
National Association of Women Business Owners - MN
http://www.nawbo-mn.org/
One Girl's Closet
http://www.onegirlscloset.com/
Women's Club of Minneapolis
http://www.womensclub.org/
Women in Networking - Minneapolis/St. Paul
http://www.mnwin.org/

My Notes

My Notes

Womens Business Development Center - MN
http://www.wbdc.org/MN/
Women's Leadership Exchange
http://www.womensleadershipexchange.com/
Women's Source
http://www.womens-source.com/

Mississippi

Executive Women International - Jackson
http://www.ewi-jackson.org/
Moms Like Me
http://jacksonms.momslikeme.com/
Professional Women's Network of Metro Jackson*
http://pwnmetrojackson.ning.com/
Clinton Career Women
http://clintoncareerwomen.ning.com/

Missouri

Missouri Womens Business Center
http://www.missouriwbc.com/

Missouri Women's Council*
http://missouriwomen.ning.com/
Powerful You
http://powerfulyou.com/
Women Owned Business Network
http://www.wobnetwork.mo.gov/

Montana

Missoula Businesswomen's Network
https://mbn.clubexpress.com/
Montana State Federation of Business & Professional Women
http://www.montanabpw.org/
Women's Leadership Network
http://www.montanabpw.org/
Women's Business Center
http://www.womenbiz.org/

Nebraska

Executive Women International - Omaha
http://www.ewi-omaha.org/
Women Supporting Women in Business
http://womensupportingwomen.ning.com/

My Notes

My Notes

Nevada

National Association of Women Busiiness Owners - Nevada
http://www.nawbosnv.org/
Nevada Womens Expo
http://www.nevadawomensexpo.com/
Womens Chamber of Commerce of Nevada
http://www.womenschamberofnevada.org/

New Hampshire

American Business Womens Association - NH
http://www.abwanh.com/
Franklin Business & Professional Womens Club
http://www.nhbpw.org/
New Hampshire Women's Policy Institute
http://www.nhwpi.org/
Southern New Hampshire Women's Business Network
http://www.snhwbn.org/
Women in Business
http://www.wbon.org/
Womens Network of the Upper Valley of NH and VT
http://www.womensnetworkuv.org/

New Jersey

Business & Professional Women - NJ
http://www.bpwnj.org/

Garden State Woman Network
http://www.gswoman.com/

Ladies Lunch
http://ladieslunch.ning.com/

National Association of Women Business Owners - Central Jersey
http://www.nawbocentraljersey.org/

National Association of Women Business Owners - Morris
http://morrisnjawbo.org/

National Association of Women Business Owners - NJ
http://www.njawbo.org/

New Jersey Association of Women Business Owners
http://www.njawbosw.org/

New Jersey Association of Women Business Owners - Mercer
http://www.njawbomercer.org/

Powerful You
http://powerfulyou.com/

Professional Women of NJ
http://pwnj.blogspot.com/

My Notes

My Notes

Shore Women
http://www.artshowandsell.com/shorewomen.html/

New Mexico

Executive Women International
http://www.ewiabq.org/ National Association of Women Business Owners - NM
http://www.nawbonm.org/
New Mexico Women in Business
http://www.newmexicowomeninbusiness.com/

New York

American Business Woman's Association - NYC
http://www.abwanyc.org/
American Business Women's Association - Niagara Falls
http://www.abwaniagara.com/
Central New York Beauties
http://centralnybeauties.ning.com/
Dinner Grrls
http://dinnergrrls.org/
Downtown Women's Club
http://www.downtownwomensclub.com

Hudson Valley Business Women's Network
http://www.midhudsonwomensnetwork.com/
Independent Business Women's Circle
http://www.ibwc.org/
Long Island Center for Business & Professional Women
http://www.liwa.org/
Long Island Women's Agenda
http://www.liwa.org/
Mohawk Valley Business Women's Network
http://www.mvbwn.org/
National Association of Women Business Owners - LI
http://www.nawboli.org/
National Association of Women Business Owners - NYC
http://www.nawbonyc.org/
Powerful You
http://powerfulyou.com/
Rochester Women's Network
http://www.rwn.org/
Rockland Business Women's Network
http://www.planet-rockland.org/RBWN/
Suffolk County Women's Business Enterprise Coalition
http://www.scwbec.org/

My Notes

My Notes

Urban Girl Squad
http://urbangirlsquad.ning.com/
Wall Street Chic
http://wallstreetchic.ning.com/
Woman Owned NY Social Network
http://womanownedny.ning.com/
Women Economic Developers of LI
http://www.wedli.org/

North Carolina

Appalachian Women Entrepreneurs
http://www.appalachianwomenentrepreneurs.org/
Business & Professional Women of Raleigh
http://www.bpwraleigh.org/
Business Women of Cherokee County
http://www.bwocc.com/
Chix in Business
http://chixinbusiness-socialnetworking.ning.com/
Diversity Woman
http://www.diversitywoman.com/

Executive Women International - Charlotte
http://www.ewicharlotte.org/
Executive Women Networking - Raleigh/Durham
http://www.ewiconnect.com/
Kerry's Network for Women
http://www.kerrysnetworkforwomen.com/
National Association of Women Business Owners - Charlotte
http://www.nawbocharlotte.org/
North Carolina Conference for Women
http://www.ncwomensconference.com/
Southern Wake Women Connections
http://swwcgroup.ning.com/
West Wake Women Entrepreneurs
http://westwakewomenpreneurs.ning.com/
Women's Business Center of NC
http://www.ncimed.com/wbc/
Women Business Owners Network of Cary
http://www.wbon-cary.org/

My Notes

My Notes

Ohio

Executive Women International - Cincinnati & Northern Kentucky
http://www.ewicincinnatinky.com/
Executive Women International - Columbus
http://www.ewicol.org/
Executive Women International - Dayton
http://www.ewiconnect.com/
Powerful You
http://powerfulyou.com/
Professional Business Women of Southeast Ohio
http://bizwomensouthwestohio.ning.com/
Tech Savvy Women
http://tswincleveland.ning.com/

Oklahoma

Executive Women International - Oklahoma City
http://www.ewi-okc.org/
Executive Women International - Tulsa
http://www.ewitulsa.org/
Ladies Who Launch - Tulsa
http://www.ladieswholaunch.com/tulsa/

National Association of Women Business Owners - Tulsa
http://www.nawbotulsa.org/
Oklahoma Women's Network
http://oklahomawomen.blogspot.com/
Women's Business Center at REI
http://www.ruralenterprises.com/womens_center.php/

Oregon

Crave Party - Portland
http://www.craveparty.com/
Executive Women International - Portland
http://www.ewi-cascade.org/
Mamapreneurs
http://www.mamapreneurs.com/
Network Women
http://www.networkwomen.org/
Women Business Network Eugene
http://www.wbneugene.org/
Women Empowering Women
http://www.wewnetwork.com/

My Notes

My Notes

Women Entrepreneurs of Oregon
http://www.oregonweo.org/
Women Entrepreneurs of Southern Oregon
http://www.wesoweb.org/

Pennsylvania

Business & Professional Women of Indiana, PA
http://www.bpwindianapa.org/
Downtown Women's Club
http://www.downtownwomensclub.com/
Executive Women International - Harrisburg
http://www.ewiharrisburg.org/
Executive Women International - Lehigh Valley
http://www.ewilehighvalley.org/
Executive Women International - Philadephia
http://www.ewiphiladelphia.org/
Executive Women International - Pittsburgh
http://www.ewipittsburgh.org/
Hershey Entrepreneurs
http://hersheyent.ning.com/

Ladies Who Launch - Philadelphia
http://www.ladieswholaunch.com/philadelphia/
National Association of Women Business Owners - Philadelphia
http://www.nawbophila.org/
National Association of Women Business Owners - Pittsburgh
http://www.nawbopittsburgh.org/
Pittsburgh Professional Women
http://www.pittsburghprofessionalwomen.com/
Powerful You
http://powerfulyou.com/
WIN
http://www.winwomen.org/
Womens Business Development Center
http://www.womensbdc.org/
Womens Business Forum
http://www.womensbusinessforum.org/
Womens Business Network of Southwestern PA
http://www.wbninc.com/
Womens Yellow Pages
http://www.philawyp.com/

My Notes

My Notes

Rhode Island

Center for Women & Enterprise
http://www.cweonline.org/
Downtown Women's Club
http://www.downtownwomensclub.com/

South Carolina

Center for Women
http://www.c4women.org/
South Carolina Women in Business
http://www.scwib.com/
South Carolina Womens Business Center
http://www.scwbc.org/
Women at Work
http://www.womenatworkinc.com/

Tennessee

Business & Professional Women - TN
http://www.bpwtn.org/

Executive Women International - Chattanooga
http://www.ewichattanooga.org/
Executive Women International - Knoxville
http://www.ewiknoxville.org/
Executive Women International - Memphis
http://www.ewimemphis.org/
Executive Women International - Nashville
http://www.ewiconnect.com/
Ladies Who Launch - Memphis
http://www.ladieswholaunch.com/memphis/
Memphis Woman Social & Professional Network
http://memphiswoman.ning.com/
National Association of Women Business Owners - Memphis
http://www.nawbomemphis.org/
Tricities Business Women Network
http://tricitiesbusinesswomen.ning.com/

Texas

American Business Womens Association - Houston
http://www.abwahouston.org/

My Notes

My Notes

Business & Professional Women of Dallas
http://www.bpwdallasinc.org/
Business & Professional Women of Texas
http://www.bpwtx.org/
Crave Party - Austin
http://www.craveparty.com/
Dallas Fort Worth Women
http://dfwwomen.ning.com/
Executive women International - Austin
http://www.austinewi.com/
Executive Women Internationl - Corpus Christi
http://www.corpuschristiewi.org/
Executive Women International - Dallas
http://www.ewidallas.com/
Executive Women International - Houston
http://www.ewihouston.org/
Executive Women International - San Antonio
http://www.ewiconnect.com/
Houston Work at Home Moms*
http://houstonwahms.ning.com/
Jewels of Houston
http://jewels12.ning.com/

Living in Style
http://livinginstyle.ning.com/
National Association of Women Business Owners - Dallas
http://www.nawbotx.org/
National Association of Women Business Owners - Houston
http://www.nawbohouston.org/
North Dallas Women in Business
http://ndwomeninbusiness.ning.com/
Outlook for Women's Networking Group
http://outlookforwomen.ning.com/
Powerful You
http://powerfulyou.com/
Professional Women's Network of Houston
http://www.pwnh.org/
South texas Women's Business Center
http://www.stwbc.com/
Texas Conference for Women
http://www.txconferenceforwomen.org/
Texas Women Partner
http://texas.womenpartner.com/

My Notes

My Notes

Texas Women's Venture Fund
http://www.texaswomenventures.com/
Women's Business Council Southwest
http://www.wbcsouthwest.org/
Women's Business Enterprise Alliance
http://www.wbea-texas.org/
Womens Business Forum
http://www.womensbusinessforum.com/
Women's Business Network
http://www.womensbusinessnetwork.org/
Women's Chamber of Commerce of Texas
http://www.womenschambertexas.com/

Utah

Executive Women International - Salt Lake City
http://www.saltlakecityewi.org/
National Association of Women Business Owners - Salt Lake City
http://www.nawboslc.org/
Park City Womens Business Network
http://www.parkcitywomensbusinessnetwork.net/
Professional Women's Network
http://www.prowomennetwork.com/

Vermont

Burlington Business & Professional Women

http://www.burlingtonbpw.org/

Mercy Connections

http://www.mercyconnections.org/

Vermont Business & Professional Women

http://www.vermontbpw.org/

Vermont Women's Business Center

http://www.vwbc.org/

Women On Top

http://womenleadvermont.ning.com/

Women in Business

http://www.wbon.org/

Womens Network of the Upper Valley of NH and VT

http://www.womensnetworkuv.org/

Womens Small Business Program

http://www.wsbp.org/

Virginia

Alexandria Professional Womens Network

http://apwn.org/

My Notes

My Notes

American Business Womens Assocaition - Richmond
http://www.richmondabwa.org/
Executive Women International - Hampton Road
http://www.ewi-hamptonroads.org/
Executive Women International - Richmond
http://www.ewirichmond.com/
Executive Women International - Roanoke
http://www.ewirichmond.com/
Ladeis Who Launch - Seattle
http://www.ladieswholaunch.com/seattle/
Lipstick Rocks
http://www.loudounwng.com/
Loudon Womens Networking Group
http://www.loudounwng.com/
National Association of Women Business Owners - Northern VA
http://www.nawbonova.org/
National Association of Women Business Owners - Richmond
http://www.nawborichmond.org/
National Association of Women Business Owners - Southeastern VA
http://www.nawboseva.org/
Network of Enterprising Women
http://www.networkofenterprisingwomen.org/

Professional Business Women's Association
http://www.pbwa.org/
Richmond American Business Womens Association
http://www.richmondabwa.org/
Richmond Women's Business Consortium
http://www.smartconnectrwbc.org/
River City Express Network
http://www.rivercityexpressnetwork.org/
Tricities Business Women Network
http://tricitiesbusinesswomen.ning.com/
Women Building & Investing in Success
http://www.wbis.biz/

Washington

Crave Party - Seattle
http://www.craveparty.com/
Crave Party - Vancouver
http://www.craveparty.com/
Executive Women International - Seattle
http://www.ewiconnect.com/
Executive Women International - Spokane
http://www.ewispokane.org

My Notes

My Notes

EXECUTIVE WOMEN INTERNATIONAL - TACOMA
http://www.ewiconnect.com/
OUR GATHERING PLACE*
http://seattlezring.ning.com/
SEATTLE WOMENS COMMISSION
http://www.seattle.gov/womenscommission/
WOMEN BUSINESS OWNERS
http://www.womenbusinessowners.org/
WOMENS BUSINESS CENTER
http://www.seattleccd.com/wbcmain/
WOMENS BUSINESS EXCHANGE
http://www.wbex.org/

West Virginia

PROFESSIONAL BUSINESS WOMENS ASSOCIATION
http://www.pbwa.org/
WEST VIRGINIA WOMENS BUSINESS CENTER
http://www.westvirginiawbc.org/

Wisconsin

Business & Professional Women - Madison
http://www.madisonbpw.com/
Executive Women International - Milwaukee
www.milwaukee-ewi.org/
Milwaukee Women
http://www.milwaukeewomeninc.org/
National Association of Women Business Owners - Madison
http://www.nawbomadison.org/
National Association of Women Business Owners - Milwaukee
http://www.nawbo-gm.org/
Wisconsin Women Equal Prosperity
http://wiweprosperity.ning.com/
Wisconsin Womens Business Initative Corporation
http://www.wwbic.com/

Wyoming

Wyoming Women's Business Center
http://www.wyomingwomen.org/

My Notes

My Notes

Showcasing Products by Women for Women

Retail space is a luxury many of us cannot afford as we venture into our own business. But our products are wonderful and deserve a voice. With the advent of the internet, women can showcase their products with a minimal investment and launch their businesses. Here are some social networking sites offering these services to women:

http://bbpnonline.ning.com/
http://divahype.ning.com/
http://www.divapreneur.com/
http://www.etsy.com/

Read All About Us

While there are many magazines, and many articles on women in business in these magazines, there a limited number of magazines dedicated to the topic of women in business. Here are the names of those print magazines along with their websites.

BRAVA
http://www.bravamagazine.com/
BUSINESS WOMAN
http://www.businesswomanmagazine.org/
DIVERSITY WOMAN
http://www.diversitywoman.com/
ENTERPRISING WOMEN
http://www.enterprisingwomen.com/
EXECUTIVE FEMALE
http://www.nafe.com/
GARDEN STATE WOMAN
http://www.gswoman.com/

My Notes

My Notes

Woman2Woman
http://www.woman2womanbusiness.com/
Pink Magazine
http://www.pinkmagazine.com/
Professional Women's Magazine
http://www.professionalwomanmag.com/
Seattle Women
http://www.seattlewomanmagazine.com/
Vermont Woman
http://www.vermontwoman.com/
Wisconsin Woman
http://www.wisconsinwomanmagazine.com/
Women's Enterprise
http://www.weusa.biz/

E-zines

E-zines are magazines that are available on the internet. The list below includes e-zines on women in business.

http://www.womenandbiz.com/

Getting Down To Business

Now that you have a list of sites for women, there are still others that you will need for your business. Instead of spending hours navigating your way through the internet, you can use this book as a roadmap for the many different topics you will need to research. While every effort has been made to organize these sites in the order you will want them, every business is different. Here is our roadmap for your reference. If you need to take a different route, just follow the topic.

Basic information is included in each category to help you understand its importance. Hints are also included to help you in the quest to launch your new venture.

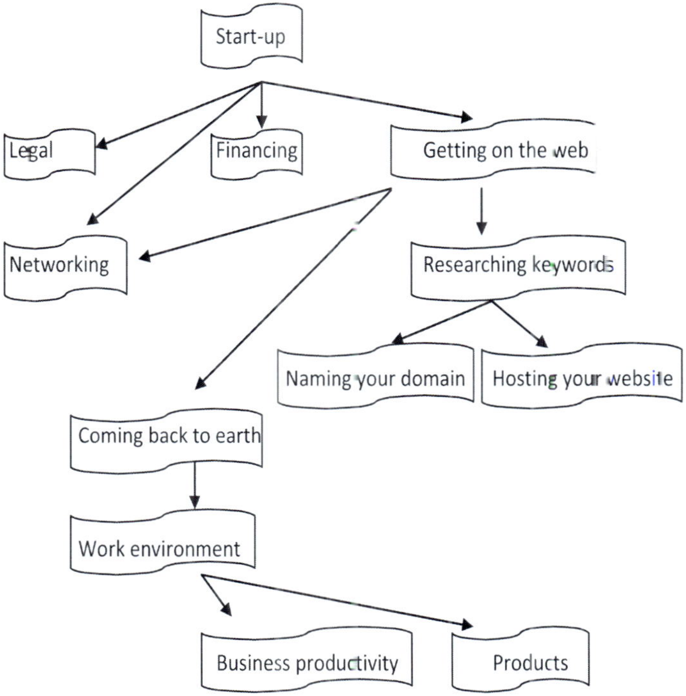

My Notes

Start Up

There are many sites available on the internet to help you get your business started. They provide how-to and training information to walk you through the business start-up process. Some sites offer personalized assistance as well. Review the offerings of each site and treat it like a menu, select the items you would like the best.

http://www.allbusiness.com/

http://www.asbdc-us.org/

http://www.askjim.biz/

http://www.businessownersideacafe.com/

http://www.buzgate.org/

http://www.enotes.com/small-business-encyclopedia/

http://www.morebusiness.com/

http://www.score.org/

http://www.smallbusinessadvocate.com/

http://www.startupnation.com/

http://www.tannedfeet.com/

http://www.toolkit.com/

http://us.smetoolkit.org/

http://www.work.com/

http://wwork.com/

★ TIP: Don't be afraid to ask for help. If you don't understand something, ask. Many of these sites offer personal assistance, webinars and more. Treat your start-up like a class, do your homework and aim for an "A".

My Notes

My Notes

Legal

As you begin to create your new business, you will need to keep government requirements in mind.

Some sites that can help with the legal forms include:

- http://www.bizfilings.com/
- http://business-law.freeadvice.com/
- http://www.businessnation.com/
- http://www.docstoc.com/
- http://www.findlaw.com/
- http://www.legalzoom.com/
- http://www.nolo.com/

If you are uncomfortable with the formalities of forming a business, an attorney and/or an accountant can help you with your decisions. File for an EIN (employer identification number) with the IRS. (http://www.irs.gov/businesses/small/article/0,,id=102767,00.html) While an EIN is for federal tax identification, some states also require their own, in addition to permits and licensing. Make sure you check your own state's site to verify. There are many websites that offer this service for a fee. While they may expedite the process for you, every state offers this information free of charge. You may need to download some forms and read through some paperwork. Here is a list of website addresses for every state.

AL	http://www.alabama.gov/
AK	http://www.dced.state.ak.us/
AZ	http://www.azcommerce.com/
AR	http://www.state.ar.us/

My Notes

My Notes

CA	http://www.calbusiness.ca.gov/
CO	http://www.colorado.gov/
CT	http://www.ct.gov/
DE	http://delaware.gov/
DC	http://www.brc.dc.gov/
FL	http://www.myflorida.com/
GA	http://sos.georgia.gov/
HA	http://www.ehawaii.gov/
ID	http://business.idaho.gov/
IL	http://business.illinois.gov/
IN	http://www.in.gov/
IA	http://www.iowa.gov/
KA	http://www.kansas.gov/businesscenter/starting/
KY	http://www.thinkkentucky.com/
LA	http://www.la.gov/

ME	http://www.maine.gov/
MD	http://www.blis.state.md.us/
MA	http://www.mass.gov/
MI	http://www.michigan.gov/
MN	http://www.deed.state.mn.us/
MS	http://www.mississippi.gov/
MO	http://www.sos.mo.gov/
NE	http://www.revenue.ne.gov/
NV	http://nv.gov/
NH	http://www.nh.gov/
NJ	http://www.state.nj.us/
NM	http://www.edd.state.nm.us/
NY	http://www.tax.state.ny.us/
NC	http://www.nccommerce.com/
ND	http://www.nd.gov/

My Notes

My Notes

OH	http://business.ohio.gov/
OK	http://www.okcommerce.gov/
OR	http://www.filinginoregon.com/
PA	http://www.paopen4business.state.pa.us/
RI	http://www.ri.gov/business/
SC	http://sc.gov/
SD	http://www.sd.gov/
TN	http://www.tennesseeanytime.org/
TX	http://www.state.tx.us/
UT	http://www.utah.gov/
VT	http://www.vermont.gov/portal/business/
VA	http://www.yesvirginia.org/startbusiness/
WA	http://access.wa.gov/
WV	http://www.state.wv.us/
WI	http://www.wisconsin.gov/state/byb/
WY	http://www.wyomingbusiness.org/

Financing

We have all heard about starting a business on a shoestring budget, but realistically, some money is needed. Your job is to determine where the money will come from. But before you can do this, you will need to complete a business plan. The business plan will help you with the financial forecasting for your business.

Money sources can include:

1. You
2. Friends and family
3. Government grants and/or loans
4. Angel investors and/or venture capitalists
5. Factoring

My Notes

My Notes

Your business plan should include:

1. Executive Summary
2. The Business
3. Market Analysis
4. Financials
    a. annual income projections
    b. a break-even worksheet
    c. projected cash flow statements
    d. a balance sheet.
5. Management Team

Some sites that offer business plan templates:

http://www.bplans.com/

http://www.myownbusiness.org/

http://www.officearrow.com/

http://www.score.org/

Some sites that offer information on financing options:

- http://www.businessfinance.com/
- http://www.fundability.com/
- http://www.guidantfinancial.com/
- http://www.venturedeal.com/

My Notes

My Notes

Networking

Congratulations! You've decided to start a business. Aren't you so excited that you want to tell the world? Then go ahead and do it. Use your social media skills. What is social media? Basically, social media is the use of technology combined with social interaction to inform. A free e-book on Social Media for Small Business can be downloaded with this link:

http://ask.officelive.com/smallbusiness/media/p/22305/download.aspx

Here are some social media sites you should know about:

http://www.delicious.com/
http://www.facebook.com/
http://www.linkedin.com/
http://www.twitter.com/

One of the major complaints about social media is the time it takes to update everything. It would be so much easier to just update your status to all of your social media sites at the same time, after all, the status is the same. Through the use of an aggregator, you can do this:

http://hellotxt.com/

http://www.ping.fm/

Twitter

Here are some applications that can make Twitter more useful in your business.

Desktop applications

http://www.desktop.seesmic.com/

http://tweetdeck.com/beta/

http://www.twhirl.com/

http://www.twittastic.net/

My Notes

My Notes

People Search:

http://nearbytweets.com/

http://www.tweetfind.com/

http://www.twellow.com/

Productivity:

http://twitpic.com/

http://twitvideo.com/

http://blip.fm/

Twitter graphics like the one used on the back cover of this book:

http://randaclay.com/freebies/free-twitter-graphics/

Getting on the Web

Moving along in your venture, you are now ready for the next step. In my opinion, this is a website. Unless your business IS website design, you do not need an expensive site, just something that you can put together and have up in a very short time (less than a day, and start to get leads from it, sell products or services on it. You will need to make a decision about what is right for you. There are:

1. websites
2. blogs
3. social networks

My Notes

Websites

Many hosting companies offer website templates. However, you can find

My Notes

templates yourself. Here are some sites that offer template designs:

http://www.freelayouts.com/

http://freesitetemplates.com/

http://www.freewebsitetemplates.com/

http://www.templatesbox.com/

http://www.templateyes.com/

Blogs

A blog is a website, an online journal. As technology advances, these sites become much more sophisticated and offer additional features through plugins and widgets.

Blog websites:

https://www.blogger.com/

http://www.bloglines.com/

http://www.wordpress.com/

TIP: The background of your blog is called a "theme". Many themes are offered for free. Premium themes may cost you, but most of them come with free support. Think about what that might be worth.

Premium themes:

http://diythemes.com/

http://headwaythemes.com/

http://www.studiopress.com/

My Notes

My Notes

There are also directories and search engines for blogs. Some of these include:

http://www.bloglines.com/

http://www.getblogs.com/

http://www.technorati.com/

Plugins add functionality to your blog. Think of it like a car. Manual transmission is standard, automatic transmission is an upgrade. Plugins are upgrades. The blog will work without them, but you can have a very sophisticated site with them. However, think of that car again. The more gadgets you add, the more things seem to go wrong. Keep your plugins under control. As you add new ones, they can disable others. Always backup your site before you add anything new, just in case!

Some wordpress plugins that are helpful to businesses:

http://wordpress.org/extend/plugins/all-in-one-seo-pack/

http://wordpress.org/extend/plugins/google-analytics-for-wordpress/

http://wordpress.org/extend/plugins/google-sitemap-generator/

Widgets are used in a blog's sidebar for "shortcuts". Unlike plugins, widgets typically do not require any customization. You can also create your own widget.

Some widget suggestions include:

Categories

Events Calendar

Links

Pages

Recent comments

Subscribe 2

Tag Cloud

My Notes

My Notes

Some widget websites:

http://www.clearspring.com/

http://musestorm.com/

http://www.widgetbox.com/

Social networks are an online grouping of people with a common interest, like a sorority, neighborhood association, special interest group, etc. These can be public or private sites. Features vary depending on the site.

Here are some sites offering social networks:

http://www.groupsite.com/

http://www.kickapps.com/

http://www.ning.com/

http://www.ryze.com/

http://www.socialgo.com/

Researching Keywords

Understanding all of the analytical aspects of keywords, SEO and the rest of the internet alphabet soup is not as important as understanding that you need them to be successful. That said, by taking advantage of the many resources available on the internet, you can create your own R&D department for your small business.

Before a product is released to the general public, the R&D department performs significant analysis to increase the odds of success. Keyword research is critical before you do anything else. Your website is actually built around keywords. As people search for your site, they usually type in a word or two to desribe what they are looking for. These are keywords. For search engine optimization, you want your keywords to help your site come up on

My Notes

My Notes

the first page. This is no easy task, and can take a long time, even with help. There are many sites out there that can help you with this process. Here is a sampling of sites (some free, so for a fee):

http://www.google.com/insights/search/
http://www.keywordcountry.com/
http://keywords.submitexpress.com/
http://keywordselite.com/
http://www.marketsamurai.com/
http://www.wordstream.com/
http://www.wordtracker.com/

Naming Your Domain

Once you have completed your keyword analysis, you should have the information you need to create your domain name. Some things to remember when naming your domain:

1. Try not to name your domain to a similar domain. Your visitors could end up on the other site.
2. Use your keywords to relate your domain name to your business.
3. Make your domain name easy to remember.
4. A shorter name is better than a long name, but initials are not good because they don't really help identify your business.
5. Try to make sure your site ends in .com. While other options are available, .com is the one most people try first.

My Notes

My Notes

Most hosting services offer domain name registration, but there are also sites that focus on domain naming. Here are some of those:

http://www.domaininform.net/

http://domain-name-ideas.com/

http://makewords.com/

http://www.nameboy.com/

http://nametumbler.com/

http://www.pickyourdomains.com/

http://www.register.com/

http://www.thesitewizard.com/

http://unique-names.com/

Now register your domain name before you lose it! You can probably do this through your hosting site, or the sites listed below.

http://000domains.com/

http://www.domain.com/

http://www.namecheap.com/

My Notes

My Notes

Hosting Your Website

Now that you have selected a name for your domain and have a list of keywords, you are ready to host your website. Hosting a website means to house, serve and maintain the files for one or more websites. Your host, the computer where your website files are stored, will assign an Internet Protocal (IP) address to your domain name to identify the online location where you've stored your files.

There are several reviews of website hosting services, so I decided to include some of them for your reference:

http://www.bestwebhosting-2009.net/
http://www.hosting-review.com/
http://www.thetop10bestwebhosting.com/

Some hosting services offer free domain registration. Here are a list of those sites:

http://www.1and1.com/
http://www.bluehost.com/
http://www.dot5hosting.com/
http://www.fatcow.com/
http://www.globat.com/
http://www.godaddy.com/
http://www.hostclear.com/
http://www.hostgator.com/
http://www.hostmonster.com/
http://www.inmotionhosting.com/
http://www.ipowerweb.com/
http://www.justhost.com/
http://www.lunarpages.com/

My Notes

My Notes

http://smallbusiness.yahoo.com/
http://www.startlogic.com/
http://www.supergreenhosting.com/
http://www.webhostingpad.com/
http://www.ixwebhosting.com/

Shared hosting sites can only accommodate a designated amount of bandwidth (the amount of information that can be transmitted over an internet connection). As your requirements exceed what is allowed, you can either increase your service or you will need to convert to a dedicated hosting server. Some sites that offer this service include:

http://www.land1.com/
http://www.bocacom.net/
http://www.codero.com/
http://www.godaddy.com/

http://www.hostgator.com/

http://www.lpdedicated.com/

http://www.ndchost.com/

http://www.peer1.com/

http://www.serverpronto.com/

http://www.superbhosting.net/

★ TIP: If you think you will need help with your hosting, select a service that offers 24/7 personal support. Call each one and ask what their support program is before you make your final selection.

My Notes

My Notes

Website Features

Maybe you have decided to design your own website. For most of us, this is a challenge. But many of the hosting companies offer free site builder templates. You just need to input your text, graphics, pictures, etc. Your host company should offer you instructions on accessing the cPanel for your website. (The cPanel is your "dashboard" to your website and is where you can control the content of your website).

The benefit of this method is that you can always change your site by changing your template and updating your text. There are many royalty free sources available that sell artwork for you to use on your website. (read the agreements carefully to ensure you are following their guidelines). The benefit to using these services is that you can usually use the artwork for printed marketing materials also, creating your own corporate identity.

Your text and page layout of your website should tell the story of your business and services. Each page can be a different chapter. Search your keywords and see what is written about topics similar to yours. Research your topic, draft an outline, and fill in the blanks. There are numerous websites that can assist you with artwork and content. (you should make sure you are using royalty free artwork) Here are some suggestions:

Artwork (includes photography and illustrations):

http://www.artzooks.com/

http://www.bigstockphoto.com/

http://www.fotosearch.com/

http://www.gettyimages.com/

http://www.illustrationworks.com/

My Notes

My Notes

http://www.imagezoo.com/
http://www.istockphoto.com/
http://www.shutterstock.com/

Content:

http://blogcontentwriter.com/
http://freesticky.com/stickyweb/
http://goarticles.com/
http://www.quickarticlepro.com/
http://www.textbroker.com/
http://www.webwisewords.com/

Flash

Flash animation can add excitement to your site when used correctly and in moderation. Flash is a technology developed by Macromedia (now owned by

Adobe) which enables animation to be stored in very small files to place on your website. While it is difficult, there are many third-party sites that make it easier to use. If you need sophisticated flash for your site you should hire a professional. For the adventurous, here are some sites to try:

http://www.123-banner.com/

http://www.show-kit.com/

http://www.swishzone.com/index.php/

http://www.wix.com/

Forms:

You can add forms to your website for your visitors to complete. These can be contact forms, request for information forms, etc.

http://formlog.com/

http://www.formsite.com/

http://freedback.com/

My Notes

My Notes

http://logiforms.com/

http://www.responders.com/

Monetizing Your Site

Once your website is up and running, you need to open the doors to the store. If you are using your website to sell products or services, you need to understand how to execute this. In order to accomplish this, you need to have three things:

1. SSL certificate

   stands for Secure Sockets Layer. It authenticates the website and its owner, while encrypting the communication between the website and its user, to ensure a level of security. An SSL certificate can usually be purchased from your hosting company as an add-on to your service. You would then have to activate it on your website.

My Notes

My Notes

2. Shopping cart

   a virtual grocery cart (of sorts) that facilitates the shopping process. Items can be added or deleted until you are ready to check-out. Features of a shopping cart can include website wizards, merchant solutions, payment options, shipping and tax configurations, statistics and security.

   Some shopping cart information:

   http://shopping-cart-review.toptenreviews.com/

3. Merchant account

   service for processing credit card payments over the internet through a payment gateway.

In addition to obtaining an SSL certificate and choosing a shopping cart option, you will also need to select a fulfillment option and a merchant solution.

Fulfillment

1. self-fulfillment
2. packaging retailer
3. professional fulfillment service
4. drop ship program

Self-fulfillment means that as you receive orders, you will package the merchandise and ship it yourself. You need to make sure that you are including packaging fees in your shipping charges. This includes packing materials, insurance and labor. You can purchase shipping materials from:

http://www.esupplystore.com/

http://www.packagingsupplies.com/

My Notes

My Notes

http://www.papermarket.com/
http://www.shippingsupply.com/
http://www.uline.com/

Packaging Retailer

There are several retailers that offer packaging and shipping services. They typically stock several different sizes of boxes, and miscellaneous packaging materials to safely package your merchandise.

http://www.theupsstore.com/
http://www.fedex.com/
http://www.usps.com/

Professional Fulfillment

As your sales escalate, you might need to outsource to an order fulfillment service. There are typically warehouse services that offer this service to their tenants. While I could list some of these here, they are generally specific to geographic locations. You should search for "shipping fulfillment services" or "warehouse fulfillment services" and speak to a select few in your area.

http://directtomarketsolutions.com/

http://webgistix.com/

http://wefulfillit.com/

Drop Ship Programs

A drop ship program is where you sell the merchandise, but it is shipped from the manufacturer under your name.

My Notes

My Notes

Affiliate Marketing

Another way to monetize your site is with affiliate marketing. You sign up with a vendor or affiliate marketer and then create a link on your website. As people click on that link and purchase an item, you make a commission on the sale (a minimum sales amount is usually required for commission).

http://www.cj.com/
http://www.clickbank.com/
http://maxbounty.com/
https://paydotcom.com/

Another option is to become an affiliate and offer your merchandise through an affiliate marketing site to other sites. This option increases your internet exposure through other sites. You would then have to pay a commission to the site that facilitates the sale of your merchandise. While posting affiliate links is usually free, there is a fee to become an affiliate.

Advertising Revenue

You can also monetize your site through advertising reverue. There are three types:

1. CPM (Cost per thousand imperssions)

   advertiser pays based on how many times an ad is seen regardless of whether or not the viewer makes a purchase. To calculate CPM, you take the cost of the ad and multiply it by 1,000 (M) and then divide that by the total traffic for the website. (for example., if a site charges $10,000 per banner and has a total audience of 250,000, the CPM is $40.)

   http://www.adbrite.com/

   http://adjungle.com/

   http://www.adsational.com/

   http://theadstop.com/

   http://www.doubleclick.com/

My Notes

My Notes

http://hyperbidder.com/

http://www.pradnetwork.com/

http://tribalfusion.com/

http://valueclickmedia.com/

2. CPC (Cost per click)

   the amount you are paid when someone clicks on an ad in your website.

   http://affiliate.com/

   http://affiliatefuel.com/

   http://leadermarkets.com/

   http://modernclick.com/

   http://www.neverblue.com/

   http://www.offerweb.net/

   http://primaryads.com/

http://www.shareasale.com/

3. CPA (Cost per action)

you are paid if the visitor buys something from the ad.

http://www.adbrite.com/

http://www.bidvertiser.com/

http://www.chitika.com/

http://www.cbprosense.net/

http://www.clicksor.com/

http://exchange.contextweb.com/

https://www.google.com/adsense/

My Notes

My Notes

Work Environment

It is very easy to get lost on the internet and forget about the basics of your business. But setting up and organizing your business is just as important. Your office environment needs to be a comfortable workspace for you. So think about the issues that can affect your workflow:

1. Layout of your room
2. Workspace on your desk
3. Color and lighting of the room
4. Storage
5. Accessibility for meeting clients
6. Sound for telephone.conference calls

You may not have thought about your home office layout when you set it up. Now that you are going to be working there on a regular basis, you need to make sure it is as comfortable as possible.

Does your desk face the door or the wall?

Are all of the items you need accessible?

Is the desk functional?

Did you choose the right room for your office?

★ TIP: Even if you are not located near a store, Ikea offers great office furniture set-ups and an online tool for room layout.

http://www.ikea.com/

My Notes

My Notes

Business Productivity

Communication

Being able to communicate with you is critical to the success of your business. But you may not always be available. Here are some communication ideas:

Avatar

an avatar is an animated speaking character, a computer user's representation of himself/herself or alter ego that can be used on your website. It is typically 3D and speaks.

http://www.codebaby.com/

http://www2.inteliwise.com/

http://www.sitepal.com/

http://www.voki.com/

Live Operator Services

Offers your online visitors an opportunity to find what they need before they get frustrated and leave your site.

http://groopz.com/

http://liveassistance.com/

http://www.livehelper.com/

http://www.liveperson.com/

http://www.upsellit.com/

http://www.websitealive.com/

Click to Call

This service provides a click-to-call button (widget) on your website. When your visitor clicks the button, they will be connected to a live operator.

http://www.boldcall.com/

http://www.clicktocall.com/

My Notes

My Notes

http://public.ifbyphone.com/

http://www.zifftalk.com/

Fax

These services enable you to receive your faxes online. You receive an e-mail notification with a link so that you can read your fax online.

http://home.efax.com/

http://www.faxaway.com/

https://www.j2.com/

http://www.myfax.com/

http://www.ringcentral.com/

http://www.trustfax.com/

http://ureach.com/

Voicemail

These services enable you to receive your voicemail online. You receive an e-mail notification with a link so that you can listen to your voicemail online.

http://www.evoice.com/

http://home.evoicereceptionist.com/

http://www.onebox.com/

http://www.ringcentral.com/

http://voicemail4free.com/

Voicemail As Text

Another option is to receive your voicemail as text in an email. Just in case you are concerned, the voicemail is also attached to the e-mail in case it is not clear in the text message.

http://www.callwave.com/

http://gotvoice.com/

My Notes

My Notes

http://jott.com/
http://phonetag.com/
http://www.spinvox.com/
http://www.voicecloud.com/

VoIP Phone Systems

VoIP is voice over internet protocol telephone service. Telephone service is received through your internet connection instead of a land line. Companies offering this service (you need to verify that their service is available in your area):

http://www.lingo.com/
http://linkshare.8x8.com/
http://www.phonepower.com/
http://www.viatalk.com/
http://www.voip.com/132/

http://www.voipyourlife.com/

http://www.vonage.com/

Skype

Skype is similar to VoIP service, but goes a little further. They offer free PC to PC phone calls. So if each of you has a webcam, you can create a live video call. Skype also offers free conference calls.

http://www.skype.com/

My Notes

My Notes

Conferencing

Conference calls have become even more important to business now that many of us work from home offices. There are different types of conference calls:

Web conferencing

Webinars

Web Conferencing

you can present information, allow you to use your computer desktop to share slides, collaborate, chat, talk and broadcast via webcam

Web conferencing services:

http://www.2gotomeeting.com/

http://www.24conference.com/

http://www.dimdim.com/

http://eagleconf.com/

http://www.freeconference.com/

http://freeconferencecall.com/

http://www.fuzemeeting.com/

http://voxwire.com/

http://www.webex.com/

Webinars

a webinar is an online seminar of sorts where you watch a video while listening on your phone; if they are on their computer, they can see whatever is being broadcast.

My Notes

My Notes

Webinar Services:

http://www.gotomeeting.com/

http://www.gotowebinar.com/

http://www.instantpresenter.com/

http://www.meetingbridge.com/

http://thewebinarpros.com/

http://www.vcall.com/

http://www.webinars.com/

http://www.webex-com/

E-Mail Marketing

One of the features you should have on your website is the ability for visitors to subscribe to it. This creates an e-mail list for you of people that are interested in what you have to offer and what you have to say. You can use this list to send periodic e-mail marketing for your business. However, since SPAM has become so prevalent, you should think about using a hosted service.

Hosted e-mail services:

- http://www.bigresponse.com/
- http://www.constantcontact.com/
- http://emaildirect.com/
- http://www.icontact.com/
- http://www.mailchimp.com/

My Notes

My Notes

Office Productivity

Since much of our time is now spent on our computers, it is increasingly difficult to break away from Twitter, not chat on Facebook and ignore LinkedIn. But, we must! The good thing is that along with social media, online productivity is becoming more popular.

Web Portals

http://www.netvibes.com/

http://www.pageflakes.com/

Project Management

http://backpackit.com/

http://www.basecamphq.com/

https://www.manymoon.com/

http://mind42.com/

http://www.mindjet.com/

http://www.mindmeister.com/

http://www.rememberthemilk.com/

http://www.smartsheet.com/

http://voo2do.com/

http://www.wrike.com/

http://www.writeboard.com/

http://www.zoho.com/

Flowchart

http://creately.com/Flowcharts-and-Workflow-Diagrams-Online/

http://www.flowchart.com/

http://www.gliffy.com/

My Notes

My Notes

Web-based Database

http://baseportal.com/

http://www.cebase.com/

http://quickbase.intuit.com/

Planner

http://iscrybe.com/

http://planner.zoho.com/

http://www.timechamp.com/

http://www.tweeto.com/

http://www.yourorganiser.com.au/

Web-based Word Processing

http://www.ajaxlaunch.com/ajaxwrite/

https://buzzword.acrobat.com/#o

http://docs.google.com/

http://www.zoho.com/

Web Productivity

http://delicious.com/

http://digg.com/

http://www.stumbleupon.com/

My Notes

My Notes

Web-based Event Management

http://www.conftool.net/

http://www.eventbee.com/

http://www.regonline.com/

http://www.reserveinteractive.com/

http://www.thriva.com/

http://www.wildapricot.com/

http://www.wingateweb.com/

Event Social Networking

http://www.eventmingle.com/

http://www.eventvue.com/

Web-Based Invitations/RSVP

http://www.anyvite.com/

http://www.evite.com/

http://events.live.com/

http://www.sendaninvite.com/

http://twtvite.com/

My Notes

My Notes

Products

Reduce time spent looking for things and increase productivity by being more organized. Determine what system will work best for you. Whether it is how your office is set-up, the filing system you are using, or your PC, explore all of the options available to you.

There are numerous products on the market, as well as web based systems, to make our lives easier and more efficient. The problem is that since we don't know they exist, we don't even know to look for them. So I am including some that focus on business productivity for your reference.

Computers

In my opinion, one of the best products on the market right now is a netbook. It is a miniature version of a laptop, with many features and a lower price tag. The disadvantages to a netbook is that is does not have a disk drive and only has 1 GB RAM. So you need to download your software from the internet or attach an external disk drive (not too much of a disadvantage).. The RAM issue is not really a problem, unless the netbook is your only PC (I am currently running WIndows 2007 and Adobe programs on mine, so it's not all that limiting).

Here are some companies to check out:

Acer	http://www.acer.com/us/
Asus	http://usa.asus.com/index.aspx/
Samsung	http://www.samsung.com/us/

My Notes

My Notes

Printers

In a home office, space is usually at a premium. Think abut consolidating items together. A printer can include a scanner, copier and fax. It can also be wireless. The amount of space a printer takes up on a desktop is called a footprint. You want to make sure your printer has a minimal footprint.

Here are some companies to check out for wireless printers:

http://www.brother-usa.com/	MFC7840W
http://www.epson.com/	Artisan 800
http://www.hp.com/	OfficeJet J4680
http://www.samsung.com/us/	ML-1630W

Productivity

https://www.getdropbox.com/home#/

http://www.filesolutions.com/

http://www.franklincovey.com/

http://www.getorganizedhere.com/

http://neatco.com/

http://www.organize.com/

http://www.pendaflex.com/

http://www.smead.com/

Printing

http://www.123print.com/

http://www.iprint.com/

http://kbp.com/

http://www.paperdirect.com/

http://www.vista.com/

My Notes

My Notes

What Does It Mean?

Affiliate Marketing	process of providing a financial incentive for other websites to promote your product or services.
Banner Advertising	a "banner" is a graphic (visual) found on a website to promote your own product or service, or sometimes somebody else's. A website with high traffic can sell that space for advertising revenue.
Blog	form of a website offering the ability to read, write or edit a shared web-based journal

C Panel	type of hosting account manager that enables you to access and modify your hosting features.
Click Through Rate (CTR)	the percentage of people that have clicked on an ad. For example, if 100 have viewed an ad, and 25 have "clicked" on it, then CTR is 25%.
CostPerClick Advertising (CPC)	cost per click (CPC) is the amount paid each time a person clicks on PPC ad.
Domain Name	the address of your website, for example, www.smallbusinessthatcould.com

My Notes

My Notes

eCommerce	buying and selling of products and services via the internet. It will require a website equipped with an SSL certificate, merchant services and shopping cart
eMail Marketing	process of obtaining e-mail addresses from people visiting your site to send regular newsletters or communication.
Hosting	service that makes your website visible on the internet. Files are stored on a host server that is permanently connected to the internet. You pay a fee for the hosting service so that your website is accessible to the public or if password protected, whoever you have given access to.

Keyword	words used to search for information relating to an assignment topic. Can be a word or phrase.
Merchant Solutions	service for processing credit card payments over the internet.
Payment Gateway	facilitates the payment process between the website and the merchant solution.
PayPerClick Advertising (PPC)	pay per click (PPC) is advertising on the internet, coded with keywords, that pays a set amount each time a person clicks on the ad.
Search Engine Optimization (SEO)	process of optimizing a website so that its ranking improves.

My Notes

My Notes

Server	a computer or other device that manages your website via a permanent connection to the internet.
Shopping Cart	a virtual grocery cart of items that facilitate the check-out process. Items can be added or deleted until you are ready to check-out. Features of a shopping cart include website wizards, merchant solutions, payment options, shipping and tax configurations, statistics and security.
SSL Certificate	stands for Secure Sockets Layer. It authenticates the website and its owner, while encrypting the communication between the website and its user, as a measure of security.

Index

My Notes

My Notes

My Notes

My Notes

My Notes

My Notes

My Notes

My Notes

My Notes